A

C000213254

# BRIEF HISTORY

# OF

# WINCHCOMBE

by Anne Crow, museum volunteer

Cover photograph by Alastair Robinson

www.winchcombemuseum.org.uk

Published by *Winchcombe Museum*

Second edition September 2021

## Acknowledgements

Many thanks to Carol Harris, Alan and Barbara Herod, and Alastair and Ruth Robinson for their invaluable help.

ISBN: 978-0-9562328-8-5

# INTRODUCTION

Winchcombe and the surrounding area have had an illustrious history with many royal connections. A powerful king of Mercia, Coenwulf (or Kenulf), was buried at Winchcombe Abbey, as was his son, a prince and a saint. Coenwulf was the only English king before the tenth century to be styled 'emperor'. At Hailes Abbey, Richard, Earl of Cornwall and King of the Romans, was buried, as well as members of his family. At Sudeley, Henry VIII's last wife, Queen Katherine Parr, is buried. Throughout the centuries, many kings, queens, bishops and archbishops have visited this corner of the Cotswolds.

Winchcombe gave its name to an extensive county, *Wincelcumbeshire*, first recorded in 1007, which comprised twelve 'hundreds' or administrative units. However, the county was incorporated into Gloucestershire in 1017. In the Domesday Book, 1086, Winchcombe was ranked as a 'burh', a fortified town, second in the county to Gloucester, which is described as a city.

This book does not claim to be a comprehensive history of the area; it seeks to tell the story of Winchcombe through buildings, or less substantial clues, that can be seen around the town or nearby. Sometimes, all that is left is a road name or a piece of carved stone; at other times, there is much of interest to be appreciated.

# CONTENTS page

Prehistoric times 6
Belas Knap 7
Roman villas 8
King Coenwulf (Kenulf) 10
Saint Kenelm 13
Winchcombe Abbey 16
The Anarchy 21
Hailes Abbey 23
Vineyard Street 25
Horse Fair 26
The George Inn 27
St Peter's Church 28
Outside the church 33
The Stocks 35
After the Dissolution 36
The Corner Cupboard Inn 37
Jacobean House 38
Chandos Street 39
Tobacco 40
Cider 41
The Workhouse 42
Fire-fighting 43
Non-conformist religious belief 45
Paper making 47
The Silk Mill 48
Winchcombe Pottery 49
Edmund Thomas Browne 50
The Town Hall 51
Abbey Terrace 53

# Prehistoric times

Millions of years ago, Winchcombe was under the sea, and fossils called **Gryphaea** are frequently found wherever people have been digging. These examples have been embedded in the wall of the Hwicci House in Hailes Street, close to the pavement.

**Gryphaea** are the fossilised remains of a type of oyster, which lived on the sea bed in shallow waters. People used to believe that these strange shapes were made as the Devil clipped his toenails, and so they are commonly known as **Devil's Toenails**. The complete fossils consist of two articulated valves: a larger gnarly-shaped shell (the "toenail") and a smaller, flattened shell, the "lid".

Fossilised ammonites and sea urchins, among other species, have also been found locally.

# Belas Knap

Among the earliest evidence of human settlement in the Winchcombe area is the late-Neolithic long barrow known as Belas Knap, meaning Beacon Hill (Old English 'bel', a beacon, and 'cnaepp', a hill top). This burial mound was probably built around 3000 B.C.

A small tribe of farmers/hunters/gatherers, living in simple houses built of wood and mud bricks, or woven hazel branches daubed with a muddy mixture, had big ideas! Instead of improving their own living standards, they designed and constructed this massive monument to house their dead. It must have taken years, probably decades, to build, but only 38 skeletons were found when it was excavated in the 1860s.

These Stone Age men used sophisticated dry stone walling and huge stones (one was 8 feet square and 2 feet thick), but they had no metal tools and the wheel had not yet been invented. What awesome determination and vision!

# Roman villas

During the Iron Age, the area now comprising Gloucestershire was within the kingdom of the tribe known as the Dobunni. It was a prosperous kingdom, relying mainly on agriculture; corn, cattle, hides etc. were exported to Gaul. There was also some trade in iron and precious metals.

When the Roman army arrived, the Dobunni soon surrendered. However, the Romans wanted to exploit their prosperity rather than destroy it, and, under Roman government, existing tribal forms of government were adapted to conform to Roman political and institutional arrangements. With an improved system of government and better roads, a highly civilised way of life was able to flourish, and many of the wealthy Romano-Britons could build villas in the Roman style. There is quite a lot of evidence that such villas were built around Winchcombe.

ROMAN PAVEMENT,
FOUND ON THE WADFIELD FARM.
FROM A DRAWING BY G. MARGILL, Esq.

Below the ground, in and around Winchcombe, there are mosaic floors and the foundations of Roman buildings. In 1863, a villa was discovered and excavated at Wadfield Farm; this villa had benefitted from the sophisticated Roman hypocaust system of underfloor heating and had this fine mosaic floor, apparently only half finished.

8

Another, even larger, villa was discovered in 1882 at Spoonley Wood, with several fine mosaics, three of which were drawn by Rev. J.H. Cardew. It is also thought probable that there are villas at Stancombe Wood and Millhampost. The probable existence of a Roman farmstead has also been established at Almsbury Farm, so this area certainly seems to have been popular with the Romano-British.

Opposite Winchcombe School, on the Greet Road, there are the remains of a villa or farm buildings which have been scheduled as an ancient monument. Perhaps the site will be excavated soon; meanwhile, the mosaic below exists to whet our appetites, hiding under a roof of corrugated iron in Spoonley Wood.

# King Coenwulf (Kenulf)

This statue was erected in St Peter's Church to honour Coenwulf, the Saxon king who chose Winchcombe to be the administrative centre of Mercia.

Under Coenwulf's rule, Mercia was the most powerful of the Anglo-Saxon kingdoms. Coenwulf was a brave warrior and a successful military commander. Furthermore, the chroniclers of the twelfth and thirteenth centuries praised him for his good government, his upholding of justice, and his piety.

He decided to build an abbey here for his final resting place. He was able to spend vast sums on the abbey and make generous endowments. A wealthy abbey was vulnerable to attack from Viking invaders, so the town was fortified. Winchcombe was the administrative centre of **Wincelcumbeshire**, but the shire was amalgamated with Gloucestershire in 1017. The Domesday Book (1086) designated it a 'burh', or fortified town; archaeological investigations in Cowl Lane and Back Lane, between 1962 and

1972, verified a ninth century defensive ditch and earth bank, which was renewed with a stone front c. 1000 A.D.

We are reminded of how important Winchcombe used to be when we read the name of the house at number 8, Hailes Street. It is called the Old Mint, because it is reputed to be on the site of the mint set up by a moneyer called Ælfnod. Housed in the British Museum and other collections, there are Winchcombe coins from the reigns of seven kings.

The silver coin above dates from c.807 A.D. with the name Coenwulf and his portrait on the obverse, minted in London.

The coin below was minted in Winchcombe towards the end of William the Conqueror's reign by Goldwine; his name is on the reverse.

At the west end of St Peter's Church (p.280, there are two stone coffins, reputed to be those of King Coenwulf and his son, St Kenelm. When part of the abbey grounds was

excavated in 1815, the coffins were found at the east end of the site of the Abbey Church of St Mary the Virgin and St Kenelm. E.T. Browne (p.50), who was present when they were found,

wrote that these two coffins were found together and *"upon removal of flag-stones which covered it (the smaller one), there appeared a skull, with a few of the other larger bones, and a very long-bladed knife, which had become a mass of rust and fell to pieces on being handled. The bones also vanished, like a vision from their sight, immediately they were exposed to air."*

Dr Phythian, who was given the coffins, told his daughter that the bodies inside appeared well preserved, even to the fleshy tints on the cheeks, but that, while the onlookers gazed, all returned to dust.

In 1895, Emma Dent (p.61) paid for the erection of the niches where the coffins rest, as well as the statues of King Coenwulf and King Henry VI.

# Saint Kenelm

Whether the coffin in St Peter's Church was Kenelm's or not, pilgrims flocked to Winchcombe to visit the shrine of the murdered prince and to taste the water at the miraculous health-giving spring at the last resting place of the cortège that brought his body home to Winchcombe. The tourists brought prosperity to the abbey, and also to the town.

It is actually estimated from surviving documents that he died in 811 or 812, in his mid-thirties, but the popular story is that he died at the age of seven, murdered in the Clent Hills by the lover of his sister, Quenthryth, so that she could take the throne. It was about 160 years later that the myth began to appear, when the monks of Winchcombe Abbey produced a Sacramentary with a brief reference to Kenelm suffering 'the agony of a martyr's death'.

Quenthryth, being a woman, would not have been allowed to take the throne, so a more likely culprit is Coelwulf, who did succeed his brother. Quenthryth was a much respected Abbess of Winchcombe, Reculver and Minster-in-Thanet.

The image on the right is taken from the well-housing on Sudeley Hill, half an hour's walk from Winchcombe, protecting Kenelm's Well. The conduit house is usually kept locked, but it is opened for his feast day on 17th July, when the well is blessed and a miracle play telling the story of the legend is enacted.

The conduit house was built in 1572 to protect Kenelm's Well.

There used to be a 16th century chapel by the well, but it was torn down in 1830, although we do have this drawing of it by Edmund T. Browne, antiquarian (p.50).

All that remains of the chapel is this 16$^{th}$ Century window in the nearby farmhouse.

In 1887, architect J. D. Wyatt rebuilt the well-head for Emma Dent of Sudeley (p.61), in honour of Queen Victoria's Golden Jubilee. He reused stones from the original chapel and placed the figure of the saint above the door. Emma Dent also paid for water to be conveyed from the well to Winchcombe; this was the town's first piped water supply (p.53). Though it looks like a small chapel, this building was used until 1930 as a pumping station.

On the inside walls there are three plaques:

This well, dating from Saxon Times Anno Domini 819, marks the spot where the body of Kenelm, 'King and Martyr', rested on the way to interment in the Abbey of Winchcombe.

A church was erected in the immediate vicinity for pilgrims attracted hither by the wonderful healing of the waters.

All that now remains of that edifice [demolished Anno Domini 1830] is a window inserted in the adjoining farm-house.

In the reign of Queen Elizabeth, Lord Chandos of Sudeley enshrined the holy well by the erection of this conduit-house, probably to commemorate one of that Queen's visits to the castle.

In this Jubilee year of Queen Victoria, June 20th, Anno Domini 1887, the sculptured figure of St Kenelm was added externally and these three legendary tablets placed therein.

In loving memory of the three brothers, John, William and the Rev. Benjamin Dent: also of their nephew John Coucher Dent, water from this abundant and ever-flowing stream was conveyed as a free gift to the inhabitants of Winchcombe by Emma, widow of the above-named John Coucher Dent. June 20, 1887

"Let thy fountains be dispersed abroad, and givers of waters in the streets" Proverbs V., 16

Oh traveller stay thy weary feet,
Drink of this water pure and sweet.
It flows for rich and poor the same.
Then go thy way, remembering still
The wayside well beneath the hill
The cup of water in His name.

# Winchcombe Abbey

Although it is true that King Coenwulf chose Winchcombe to be his administrative centre because of its geographical position, it was the abbey he founded which first raised Winchcombe to prominence. For more than 700 years, the abbey gave Winchcombe status and brought it prosperity, and, when the abbey fell, so did the town.

Winchcombe Abbey is thought to have been added to a convent of nuns established by King Offa in 787. It was dedicated to St Peter in 811 by Wulfred, Archbishop of Canterbury, in the presence of Cuthred, King of Kent; Sired, King of the East Saxons; as well as all the great men of the kingdom of Mercia. It was in 970 that the abbey was rededicated under Benedictine rule.

The abbey was very well endowed; it was originally intended to house a community of 300 monks and servants, and Coenwulf granted them more than 13,000 acres to support the community. Wealthy people made significant donations to ensure a place in heaven, and, by 1095, the abbey controlled more than 25,000 acres. Such an important abbey inevitably attracted royal visitors to the town. In 942, the abbey hosted a 'witenagemot' (a national council or parliament) held by King Edmund the Magnificent, attended by Archbishop Wulfstan of York and other bishops and earls. King Ethelred the Unready used to hunt here in his royal deer park. In 1144, King Stephen defeated Roger, Earl of Hereford, outside Winchcombe and made the town his headquarters. King John stayed here in 1198, 1207 and 1208.

When Henry III and his entourage came to Hailes for such ceremonies as the dedication of Hailes Abbey and the arrival of the relic of the Holy Blood, they stayed at Winchcombe. In 1264, Henry was captured at the Battle of Lewes and kept prisoner on parole in Winchcombe Abbey. It is known that King Edward I visited Winchcombe in 1290, 1294 and then, with Queen Margaret, in 1301 for the funeral of his cousin, Edmund, Earl of Cornwall. Edward III visited in 1327 and Edward IV in 1461.

In 1534, the Act of Supremacy was passed, naming Henry VIII as head of the church in England. Thomas Cromwell was appointed the king's vicar general, with powers to visit and reform all monastic institutions. He visited the abbey in 1535 and set a zealous protestant, Anthony Saunders, to lecture the monks and undermine the authority of the abbot, in preparation for dissolution.

Four years later, Winchcombe Abbey was dissolved. The abbey and manor of Winchcombe were granted to Sir John Bridges, Constable of Sudeley, and later to Sir Thomas Seymour by Edward VI. Most of the stone was taken to Sudeley to rebuild the castle, but there are some pieces of decorative stone to be found in houses and gardens around Winchcombe. A lot of abbey stone was used in the building of the Corner Cupboard Inn (p.37) and the carved rabbits and flowers on the wall of 94 Gloucester Street were probably once part of the Abbey.

Abbot Richard Kidderminster's scholarly history of the abbey was taken to London, where it perished in the Great Fire of 1666 (p.27). There is no surviving drawing of the abbey, but artists have used the research of historians to help them imagine what the abbey might have looked like.

The model above, researched by John Stevinson, drawn by Ronald Green and built by Mac Yates, is in St Peter's Church. The painting below, by Martin Podd, imagines how the abbey church would have looked next to St Peter's Church during the seventy or so years after St Peter's was built (p.28).

## The Abbot's House

When the abbey was dissolved, only the religious buildings were demolished, so the Abbot's House survived.

In 1746, Winchcombe's vestry leased the building to use it as a workhouse where the poorest inhabitants of Winchcombe could be accommodated and given some employment (p.42). However, in 1814, the owners decided to serve an eviction order, for the removal of the residents, on the grounds that the house was dilapidated beyond repair. Despite the historical value of the building, the owners went ahead with the demolition. Edmund Thomas Browne made a record of the building in the two sketches above.

The building now known as Abbot's House [5 & 7 High Street] was probably associated with the pilgrim's hostel at the George, perhaps as a house for the abbey's servants who managed the hostel. On the wall is a carved angel, supporting the abbey's coat of arms.

## Sheep

Sheep-farming was the main source of the abbey's cash income. The Cotswolds had a thriving woollen industry from the end of the eighth century, exporting raw wool, as well as woollen cloaks and blankets, to the continent. The wool from the breed known as the Cotswold Lion was highly prized, and Florentine merchants bought large quantities of the shiny, linen-like wool. It was woven together with fine wires of real gold, to make ceremonial garments for priests and kings.

The land was owned by either the abbey or the lord of Sudeley, and people paid to work a strip of land, defined by the 'acre'; this was the amount one person could plough in one day's work, using a team of oxen pulling a wooden plough. The plough blade cut the turf and forced the soil against a board, which turned it over and moved it sideways.

At the end of the field, the oxen would loop round to come back down the field to pile the soil against the first cut. By going round your land in this manner the effect was to push the soil in towards the middle and create a long heap with a larger surface area and better drainage. Temporary barriers would be set up to keep cattle out of the fields, but, after the crop was harvested, the land would revert to common land for sheep grazing. Remains of this strip-farming survive as the 'ridge and furrow' undulating pastures in the fields outside the town.

# The Anarchy

When Henry I died in 1135, his nephew, Stephen, claimed the throne, but Henry's daughter, Matilda, refused to accept this, and, for nineteen years, until Stephen died, there was civil war in England, a time known as the 'Anarchy.'

**Postlip Chapel**

No doubt for the protection of his estate, John of Sudeley fortified Sudeley Manor during Stephen's reign. John supported Matilda, while Abbot Robert of Winchcombe supported Stephen. Not surprisingly, Winchcombe was in the thick of the fighting. The king and Matilda's half-brother, Robert, Earl of Gloucester, fought to control the town. The Chapel of St James at Postlip was built at this time by the lord of the manor, William de Solers, so that his tenants would not have to risk their lives travelling to the nearest church at Winchcombe.

During the religious upheaval in the 16th century, the chapel was defiled, but it was restored to Catholic worship in 1891, after being used as a sheep pen.

## Hailes Church

Also during Stephen's reign, Ralph of Worcester decided to fortify a castle at the small hamlet of Hailes, and he also built a church there. Because Hailes belonged parochially to Winchcombe Abbey, Abbot Robert resisted Ralph's demands that the church at Hailes should have the right to bury the dead. Taking advantage of the lawlessness in the country, Ralph blockaded the abbey and starved the monks until they agreed to concede the right of burial.

Hailes Church was particularly important because the Cistercian order did not allow visitors, however royal, into the abbey church.

### Fire

Presumably hoping for protection from the Anarchy, many Winchcombe residents had built flimsy wattle and daub cottages with thatched roofs around the abbey on all sides. When fire broke out in 1151, the abbey buildings, including the church, were substantially destroyed.

# Hailes Abbey

In 1245, Henry III granted his brother Richard, Earl of Cornwall, the manor of Hailes to allow him to build an abbey to fulfil a vow made when he was in danger of drowning. As well as paying for the abbey to be built and dedicated, Earl Richard richly endowed the abbey so that the monks could spend their days praising, praying and studying, as well as looking after the sick, the old and the poor. Throughout the life of the monastery, rich people continued to give land, money and other gifts to the monks. Their coats of arms can be seen in tiles or carved in stone in the abbey museum.

Among them, there are examples of tiles bearing the double-headed eagle, familiar as the arms of the German Emperor. Richard was elected Holy Roman Emperor by four out of seven German princes in 1256; however, the Pope refused him use of the title, so he was crowned King of the Romans by the Archbishop of Cologne. He died in 1272 and was buried at Hailes, almost certainly in the presbytery, close to the high altar. His second wife, Sanchia of Provence, was buried there in 1261, and also three of Richard's sons.

In 1270, Edmund, their younger surviving son, gave the abbey a phial of the Holy Blood of Christ, guaranteed as authentic by the Patriarch of Jerusalem, later Pope Urban IV. King Henry III, his wife, Queen Eleanor, and a great many nobles and bishops attended the consecration of the abbey in 1251, as well as the ceremony accompanying the arrival of the relic.

A relic as precious as the Holy Blood demanded a worthy setting, and so the whole east end of the church was rebuilt and extended. The form this new building took was that of a coronet of chapels radiating from an ambulatory around an apse. This design, known as **chevet**, is rare in English churches.

The relic was enshrined on a platform behind the high altar. The fact that the blood was proved in the sixteenth century to be fake does not diminish its importance to those believers who flocked to Hailes in their thousands to have their sins forgiven and, in some cases, to be cured.

In 1535, Henry VIII and Anne Boleyn visited Winchcombe Abbey, and Anne is said to have sent chaplains to Hailes to enquire into the *"abominable abuse"* of pilgrimage. In 1538, the relic was denounced as being nothing more than duck's blood. Commissioners examined it, declared it to be an unctuous gum and took it to London. On Christmas Eve, 1539, the abbot and monks signed a document surrendering the abbey to Henry's commissioners, and the abbey was effectively demolished. The Abbot's House, however, remained, and it became the residence of the Tracy family until early in the eighteenth century, when it was abandoned to fall into ruin. A century later, the site of the abbey was excavated by Welbore St Clair Baddeley.

# Vineyard Street

In the late eleventh century, climate change caused the average temperature of Western Europe to rise, and it seems that Winchcombe Abbey had a vineyard on the south-facing slope down towards the river. The first reference to Vineyard Street (Le Winzardstret) is in 1320 when Matilda of Sydenham was granted a corrody by the abbey entitling her to live in one of the houses. In 1500, it was recorded as Wyneyarde Street.

In 1891, the ford over the River Isbourne was replaced by a bridge, at the behest of Emma Dent. During excavation for the foundations, John Oakey, the builder, found the stump of the town's ducking stool, used to punish scolding women. This explains why the street was once called Duck Street.

Three of the cottages have a Mansard roof, named after the seventeenth century French architect who designed it. As the cottages are older, it is probable that this design offered a simple way to add another storey, without requiring extra stone.

# Horse Fair

Abbot Ralph (1184 – 1194) granted a parcel of land to the abbey's sacristy which is thought to have been for a horse market. From then until the Great War, Winchcombe was well known  for its horse fairs, and people would travel great distances to buy horses here. You can still see many of the rings to which they were tethered; bushes were also displayed on the rings to advertise freshly brewed ale.

"The whole of North Street was full of horses tied up as close as they could stand, while the side lanes, and some distance of the Greet and Gretton Roads, were practically blocked. ... Undoubtedly the July Fair was the most noted one, for on the 12th July, 1254, King Henry III, who was staying at Windsor at that time, sent to the Burgesses of Winchcombe to assist his stewards ... in purchasing horses." (**Reminiscences of Winchcombe**, John Oakey, 1937)

# The George Inn

Peek inside the main door of the former George Inn, and you will see this pilgrims' gallery, and underneath it is a stone bath in which pilgrims would have cleansed themselves before going to the shrine of St Kenelm. The George was converted to housing units in 1988, so please respect the privacy of residents if you venture through the door to see the gallery.

The George was a small coaching inn before it was acquired by Abbot Richard Kidderminster early in the sixteenth century to accommodate pilgrims. The Abbot's initials are carved on the spandrels on either side of the main entrance to the George. His initials can also be found on the abbey door now kept in St Peter's Church.

Under Abbot Kidderminster, Winchcombe Abbey was known as a prestigious centre of learning. Henry VIII described him as 'a man of remarkable learning and experience', and, in 1512, the king sent him as an ambassador to Pope Julius II. The Abbot compiled a register including everything he could find out about the abbey's history. After the dissolution, this valuable document passed into the hands of a high court judge and was destroyed in the Great Fire of London (p.17).

# St Peter's Church

The present building was constructed in the middle of the fifteenth century, replacing the original church which was in a dangerous state. Unusually, it was completed within ten years. It is not technically a wool church, since the proceeds of the wool trade went to the

Drawing by J. Drayton Wyatt before 1872 restoration

abbey. The abbot paid for the rebuilding of the chancel; the parishioners raised £200, which probably paid for the nave and the tower, and Lord Ralph Boteler of Sudeley rescued the project when the money ran out.

The original stained glass was probably removed during the reign of Edward VI when all vestiges of Roman Catholicism were being swept away. Some fragments, however, including these angels, were found in the porch room in 1928 when Eleanor Adlard was setting up her Folk Museum.

During the civil wars between the King and Parliament, Sudeley was besieged twice, and the town was plundered by Parliamentary soldiers, as well as a vicious royalist party from Chipping Campden. Probably at the time of the second siege in 1644, more extreme residents invited a radical preacher, Carne Helme, to take charge of St Peter's. The church furnishings were changed to reflect more extreme Protestant ideas.

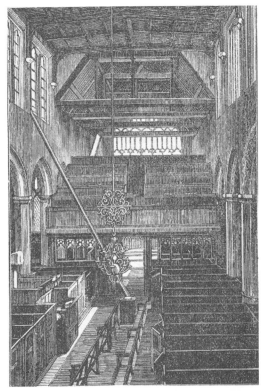

These lasted until the renovation of the church, 1870-3, when the present more traditional, Anglican furnishings were installed. This drawing shows the interior of the church before its refurbishment. The clerestory was carried through to the east end of the chancel. The Flemish candelabrum in the nave was given in 1753 by John Merryman, a churchwarden and bailiff.

The rood screen carved in the fifteenth century survives; make sure you look for the famous Winchcombe Imp. You might also like to look for the masons' marks, scratched or chiselled onto the stones to make sure the mason was paid for his work. Interestingly, some of the same marks which are found at St Peter's, are also found in St Mary's Church, Sudeley, and the old church at Gretton.

Protected by a curtain, there is a fascinating altar frontal found in a coal-hole in the 1840s. It was constructed by sewing together panels of a redundant fourteenth century clerical mantle and then adding a Tudor border in  fishbone style. Because there are pomegranates, the emblem of Queen Katherine of Aragon, embroidered on the border, tradition holds that she and her ladies sewed this altar cloth.

The panels are populated by delightful figures of saints and angels, and in the centre is a crucifix, the body of which is missing. Curiously, this missing piece was found in the embroideries of Minsterworth Church when both pieces were being repaired at the same time at the Royal School of Needlework. Apparently, ladies had been permitted to cut pieces off to use as patterns for their embroidery.

Above the altar cloth is a plaque commemorating the seven Winchcombe men who gave their lives for their country in the Boer War in South Africa at the beginning of the twentieth century.

The magnificent east window, made by Hardman & Co of Birmingham, is unique, not just for its subject matter, but also because the whole window, including the tracery, depicts one picture. The window does not merely represent the Bible story of Christ walking on the Sea of Galilee and St Peter trying unsuccessfully to emulate him; it also has symbolic significance. A ship represents the Christian Church sailing through all perils, and the fish in the water represent the believers. The initial letters of the Greek words *'Jesus Christ, Son of God, Saviour'* spell the Greek word for 'ichthys', a symbol which looks like a fish, so a fish was adopted by early Christians as a secret way to declare their faith.

In the bottom right hand corner of the window in the north-west corner of the church is a tiny image of a friar. The window was made in 1906 by the Whitefriars Glass Company, sited between Fleet Street and the River Thames, in London. This small glassworks is believed to have been established in 1680. It gained its name and its rebus (or logo) because Carmelite monks once lived on the site.

The firm was bought by James Powell, a wine merchant, in 1834. When his sons took over after his death, Arthur Powell opened a department for stained glass to meet what was now a growing demand.

Most of the other stained glass windows in St Peter's Church were made by this company, before they adopted the rebus.

The three eighteenth century lights in the Lady Chapel were installed in 1875 and the nineteenth century stained glass in the clerestory was brought from Sudeley Castle in 1878.

An organ was purchased in 1782; the central panel is said to have been carved by Grinling Gibbons. Another organ, bought in 1877, was amalgamated with it in 1890.

# Outside the church

To the right of the west door of St Peter's Church, there is a wedge-shaped flower trough. At the wide end, there is a cross carved on the side of it. According to Reverend Meurig-Davies, the trough was placed in this position in 1934, but he does not say where it came from.

In 2016, when the flower trough had been emptied before being refilled with new plants, part of it was turned over for inspection and photographing. The flower trough has drain holes, but they are likely to be of a modern date. It could be a very rare form of coffin lid; however, on what would have been the top surface, there is no sign of any carving. Also, the trough has a raised headrest which indicates it might possibly have been the coffin base of a very slim person.

The distinctive golden cockerel that watches over the town from the top of the 90 foot tower was lent to St Peter's Church by St Mary Redcliffe Church in Bristol, on the understanding that it would be offered back if ever it was decided that it was no longer needed.

There are about forty grotesques high on the walls outside the church. About half of them depict devils and the rest seem to be caricatures of people known to the stone masons, such as the master mason holding his hammer, now broken off.

The figure on the left is thought to be Ralph Boteler, looking much happier than he was in 1465 when he was arrested and imprisoned in the Tower of London until he agreed to 'sell' Sudeley to King Edward IV. Ralph had always been a loyal supporter of King Henry VI of Lancaster (p.54).

# The Stocks

You may remember Winchcombe's stocks standing under John Oakey's canopy outside the Town Hall, but they have had to be moved inside to preserve them.

Stocks were used as a punishment from the early middle ages up to the nineteenth century. They were originally intended as a means of confining offenders once they had committed a crime; however, they were eventually used as a means of punishment in themselves. After the Black Death in 1341, the scarcity of labour resulted in the **Statute of Labourers** in 1351, which threatened that those who refused to work would be put in the stocks and branded. In 1405, an Act of Parliament instructed every town and village to have a set of stocks. Without them, a village was downgraded to hamlet status. This Act has never been repealed!

Winchcombe's stocks, with its seven holes, were still in use as late as 1860, when a man was put in them for the crime of drunkenness. They provided a popular form of entertainment, right in the centre of town, as public humiliation was a major part of the punishment. Offenders would be stuck there in all weathers, often for long periods of time, and people could throw whatever revolting things they liked at the helpless miscreants. There is speculation that, when the stocks were built, there must have been a persistent one-legged offender; however, only one foot needs to be secured.

# After the Dissolution

When the abbey was dissolved in 1539 (p.17), the monks were given pensions or found other positions, but the numerous abbey servants lost their jobs. Pilgrims stopped coming to the town. Traders stopped bringing their goods to sell. Craftsmen lost their best customers. There was no-one to organise the wool trade. There were no handouts to the poor, no education for people's sons, no formal health care. This prosperous and important town fell into a decline.

Lady Dorothy Chandos of Sudeley brought the town's plight to the attention of Queen Elizabeth when she received a royal visit. In 1575, the Queen awarded Winchcombe a charter, granting the privilege of holding an annual three-day fair in April, a weekly market on Tuesdays and a 'pie powder court' at which disputes could be settled quickly on fair days.

More tangible evidence of the philanthropy of Lady Dorothy is provided by the alms-houses, built in 1573 between Queen's Square and Mill Lane to accommodate twelve poor women. The Chandos coat of arms is badly eroded.

# The Corner Cupboard Inn

The Corner Cuboard Inn was built in the middle of the sixteenth century as a farmhouse, using some stone from the ruins of the abbey.

By 1759, it was no longer a farmhouse but a gentleman's residence owned by John Durham, paper manufacturer, who left the house to his daughter, Mary. The building did not become an inn until 1872, when the first licence was granted to William Richardson, who was the licensee when this photograph was taken. John Oakey, a local builder, recalled that one of the regular customers, John Greenhalf, jokingly named the pub, because, at that time, almost every angle of the house had a built in corner cupboard.

The bust of Benjamin Disraeli above the front door has adorned the pub since at least 1924, when a booklet called *'Gloucestershire Inns'* was published, mentioning it.

# Jacobean House

The Chandos Alms-houses and Jacobean House were built on the site of a castle which was referred to in 1393 as 'Ivy Castle', presumably because it was, by that time, dilapidated and covered in ivy. John Leland saw the ruins of it when he visited the town in 1540 or 1541.

After the loss of the abbey, there was no formal education in Winchcombe, so Jacobean House was built in 1618 to house the King's School. The school-room occupied the entire ground floor; the school-master had a self-contained flat on the first floor, with a separate entrance at the back, and there were dormitories for the boys on the second floor.

When other arrangements were made for education, the corporation rented out Jacobean House for an attorney's office, a savings bank etc. However, when it was decided to rebuild the Town Hall, the house was sold to John Coucher Dent to help repay the debts, and then, in 2000, it was sold to a private buyer.

# Chandos Street

There is a local tradition that a Saxon church of St Nicholas was situated at the junction of Bull Lane and Chandos Street, formerly known as St Nicholas Street. Tradition holds that the building was only demolished late in the nineteenth century when it was being used as a cart shed; however, according to John Leland, who visited the town in 1540/41, "*There was of ancient tyme a church of St Nicholas in the East part of the Towne, decayed many years since*".

Chandos Street gained its name in 1621 when Lady Dorothy's daughter-in-law, Lady Frances Chandos, provided money for the Chandos Grammar School for 14 children. In 1876, the school was merged with the King's School and moved into a new building in Chandos Street. The school closed in 1907, and, following a brief period as a working men's club, the buildings were bought by Mrs Elizabeth Forster of Postlip Hall in 1915. The new school building was adapted for Catholic worship, and the original school building (see above) was converted for use as The Presbytery (the Priest's House). This building was demolished in the 1960s and replaced by a modern house set back from the road.

Lady Chandos' endowment continues in the Chandos Exhibition Foundation, providing financial help for educational purposes to individuals or schools in the Winchcombe district.

# Tobacco

One initiative which did make a difference was John Stratford's decision in 1619 to grow tobacco. Tobacco Close was built on land known as Tobacco Piece, so it probably was grown here. However, it was grown widely in the Winchcombe and Cheltenham area for about seventy years. A proclamation was issued in 1619 making tobacco-growing illegal in order to protect the Virginia trade, and Stratford turned to growing flax, but others did not give up. Petitions were rejected, but people were desperate, so there were riots whenever an attempt was made to destroy the crop. When, in 1667, an army of 120 horse of the King's and Duke's Guards were sent to cut down the tobacco, even they were driven off.

Constable Nicholas Robinson filed a report in 1676 that he was roughly handled, his wife and children threatened and persecuted by his fellow townsfolk, because he tried to do his duty. The irony is that there was less crime because poor people did not need to beg, steal, or pull hedges for firewood, as they could work in the fields or grow tobacco in their gardens. Tobacco-growing died out in the 1680s because the land had been intensively farmed for so long that it was exhausted, and, also, the price of the superior crop in Virginia fell.

# Cider

Another crop that used to be grown extensively in this area was cider apples. In this area, cultivation probably started with the Romans, who brought a plethora of apple varieties, orcharding techniques and cider-making knowledge.

In the nineteenth century, many local people would take their

cider apples to Bill Summers' cider press, made in 1890, which now stands outside the library. The demand for housing, and the nation's agricultural policies, have decimated the orchards around the town, and the manufacture of cheap mass-produced carbonated cider has priced local cider out of the market.

Even a hundred years ago, Winchcombe had orchards in the centre of town as well as in the surrounding countryside. However, cider apples were not usually a cash crop. Cider was made for home consumption, and workers would expect cider as part of their wages. During harvest, they would carry a wooden keg holding a gallon of cider attached to their belts to rehydrate them as they worked throughout the day.

# The Workhouse

It was in March 1745 that Winchcombe's vestry first decided to set up a workhouse in the town, where the poorest inhabitants could be accommodated and given employment to defray the cost of public provision. They leased the Abbot's House (p.19). When the owners of the house demolished it in 1815, the workhouse was re-established in a former Malthouse at the foot of what is now Bicks Lane.

When the Poor Law Amendment Act was passed in 1834, responsibility for poor relief was transferred to the Board of Guardians for the Winchcombe Poor Law Union. A new, purpose-built workhouse for the town and surrounding parishes was constructed to the west of Malthouse Lane. This gateway on Gloucester St. was an entrance to the site.

When it was no longer needed, the building became a boys' home and then a youth centre before it was demolished in the 1950s. The site was then developed for purpose-built dwellings for elderly people.

# Fire-fighting

Winchcombe's first fire engine, procured in 1789 through voluntary contributions, was housed in St Peter's Church. In 1846, it was moved to the Booth Hall, next to the Town Hall (p.51).

When the Town Hall was rebuilt and enlarged in 1853, a new fire station was built in Chandos Street. The housing for the siren can still be seen on the roof.

In 1891, when Emma Dent had provided the town with piped water, a new fire engine was bought.

By 1940, the station was too small for the more modern fire engines, so the present station was built in Gretton Road.

On the walls of a number of old houses in Winchcombe may be seen these metal plaques or badges, erected by insurance companies to signify that the property was insured with them. If the property did not display the appropriate plaque, it was left to burn.

Each company was identified by its emblem embossed upon the plaque. Earlier ones were cast in lead and had a number corresponding to the number of the insurance policy engraved on a panel beneath the symbol. These are usually referred to as fire marks. The Sun Fire Office was established in 1710.

The Phoenix Company was started in 1782; the phoenix is a mythical bird, symbolising renewal and hope, which is reborn from the ashes of its predecessor. Later plaques, known as fire-plates, were usually pressed out of thin copper-plate, or tinned sheet-iron. These were often highly coloured for they also acted as advertisements.

Fire insurance was expensive; only wealthy people could afford it, so it is unlikely that any of the plaques in the town were actually erected in the eighteenth century.

# Non-conformist religious belief

During the latter part of the eighteenth century, the practice of non-conformist belief began to develop vigorously in the Winchcombe district. So vigorous was Winchcombe's Methodism that it supplied preachers for Cheltenham, and a Winchcombe circuit was founded in 1812; people walked into town from many of the surrounding villages, brought their families and their lunch, and spent the day in town, returning home when the afternoon service was over.

The Rev John Wesley (1703-91) stayed here in the home of a Methodist John Staite in 1755 and 1779 whilst Preaching in the Town.

On the wall of the Wesley House, to the left of the door, is a plaque commemorating the fact that John Wesley stayed there. John Wesley was a theologian and preacher, one of three men who founded the evangelical movement known as Methodism. He visited this area on many occasions between 1739 and 1779, and stayed at the house of John Staite.

Baptists were also active here in the early nineteenth century. The Baptist Chapel was opened in 1811 in the High Street. It is now used as the Guide Hall.

**Methodist Chapel 1810**

The Methodist Chapel was built in 1810, in Cowl Lane. It could accommodate more than 200 worshippers, with a singers' gallery and space for an orchestra.

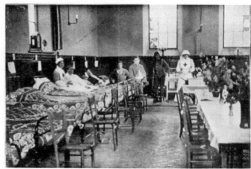

When the present chapel in the High Street was opened in 1885, this building became an infants' school, then a VAD Hospital ward during the First World War.

It has since served as the Women's Institute Hall and then Winchcombe Parish Hall, before being converted to private housing in 2015.

**Methodist Church 1885**

46

# Paper making

Since 1982, Hollingsworth and Vose have been manufacturing advanced filtration materials at Postlip. However Postlip Upper Mill has a long history. There were two watermills recorded at Postlip in the Domesday Book. This one produced corn until the 1720s, when John Durham took it over and converted the mill to paper production.

In the 19$^{th}$ and 20$^{th}$ centuries, the paper mill was a major employer in the town. Paper-making was a laborious process, largely carried out by hand. Linen and cotton rags had to be sorted, cut into small pieces and converted into pulp. The pulp was produced by beating the rags on an iron platen with an iron-shod wooden mallet.

In 1850, James Robert Evans and his partner, William Gates Adlard, became tenants. They were making a varied selection of papers which required special processes and dyes which had to be prepared from some very noxious substances, making the mill an unpleasant place to work. All the dirt from the rags, the bleach residue and surplus chemicals, together with refuse, was all dumped into the River Isbourne!

In 1876, Evans, Adlard & Co purchased the mills and started a major rebuilding programme to modernise the mills. However, after the Second World War, the invention of the ballpoint pen led to a fall in demand for blotting paper. Production of blotting paper ceased in 1969, and most of Postlip's business was then making filter papers for the motor industry and laboratory work.

# The Silk Mill

This plaque is attached to the wall on the corner of Castle Street and Silk Mill Lane. In 1827, Edward Banbury converted a three-storey building from a corn mill to a silk mill, using water-powered machinery to throw or twist the delicate silk into usable threads and wind it onto bobbins.

Unfortunately, it did little to relieve poverty in the town as it was worked chiefly by child labour, mostly badly paid little girls, some as young as eight, who risked accidents in the machinery. By 1850, the business was large enough to support a hundred employees, and it was one of the largest employers in the town. However the mill closed down in 1855, probably due to a surge of imports from France.

The mill was demolished in 1872, and the stone was used to build the Congregational chapel, now known as Encounter Church, in Gretton Road. A cornerstone, dated 1763, is in Winchcombe Museum. It was Thomas Swinburne of Corndean Hall who arranged for this imposing church to be built on the site of a large cider barn.

The boys' school, opposite the church, was built in 1883, and it continued to provide education for older boys until 1952.

# Winchcombe Pottery

 Winchcombe Pottery's magnificent bottle kiln has been at the Pottery on Beckett's Lane since early in the nineteenth century, when there was a utilitarian pottery, catering for local needs, on the site. Richard Beckett, the potter, died in 1913, and the First World War took the young men away in 1914, so the pottery closed. The house and buildings were sold to Mr Butler, a local farmer, in 1923.

Michael Cardew, who wanted to revive traditional slip-wares, saw the derelict pottery in 1926 and arranged to rent it, re-opening as Winchcombe Pottery. Two years later, he had a very successful exhibition in London which put Winchcombe Pottery on the map, earning it national and international acclaim.

The bottle kiln, however, has not been used since 1953, when a seam of sulphates in the local clay caused very serious problems. While the team, led by Ray Finch, tried to identify the trouble, an electric kiln was installed in Chandos House, Winchcombe, until electricity was supplied to the pottery, and, in 1956, a small stoneware kiln adapted to oil firing was acquired. Gradually, Winchcombe Pottery got back on its feet, and it is still making Winchcombe famous throughout the world. Visitors to the pottery can see the kiln as well as make purchases from a wide range of hand thrown pots.

# Edmund Thomas Browne

E.T. Browne was Winchcombe's High Bailiff from 1845 until his death in 1859 and, as his obituary stated, *"during that period has won for himself the universal admiration, gratitude and respect of his fellow townsmen."* Those who are now interested in Winchcombe's history are grateful for his drawings of buildings which were demolished in his life-time.

We owe him for the pictures of the Abbot's House (p. 19) and St Kenelm's Chapel (p. 14), and also for the chapel at Greet (right) and an old monastic house on the corner of High Street and North Street (below). He rescued the carved barge-board which now hangs in the museum.

GREET CHAPEL. FROM A SKETCH BY E. T. BROWNE, Esq., BEFORE IT WAS FINALLY DEMOLISHED ABOUT 1815

He also observed and recorded significant events in the town's history, such as the exhumation of Katherine Parr's coffin, and, in 1837, the first carriages to use the newly straightened section of road next to the *"recently formed spacious walk in the town called Abbey Terrace"*.

# The Town Hall

TOWN HALL AND HIGH STREET, WINCHCOMBE.

The Guildhall and Booth Hall are first mentioned in a twelfth century document; at this time, they seem to have been separate buildings. The Guildhall, in North Street, would have provided a meeting place for leading townspeople and accommodation for important civic ceremonies, while the Booth Hall, in the High Street, provided a covered market.

By 1680, it seems that they occupied one building, with the town hall on the first floor and the market hall on the ground floor. Petty offenders were kept in the cellar, the bridewell, but, by 1776, when John Howard, the prison reformer, visited Winchcombe, they were being housed in the garret, in appalling conditions, in a building which was "*quite out of repair*". However, in spite of its dangerous condition, the

Town Hall was still being used for theatrical entertainments and other assemblies.

The present building was erected in 1853 on the same site. The ground floor was still the market place, and the rails, from which meat and sausages were hung, can still be seen. The room upstairs continued to be used for concerts, plays, dances, sales, meetings and lectures, and it also housed the Magistrates' Court. In 1871, a new wing was added to provide a magistrates' retiring room upstairs and a waiting room downstairs.

In 1891, the corporation was replaced by a directly elected rural district council, and the Town Hall was put in the hands of a newly established Town Trust, which now uses it to house Winchcombe Museum.

The Town Hall clock was presented to Winchcombe in 1897, by Reginald H. Prance. After more than 100 years, it had to be taken down in 2000, because the heavy face had become dangerous. The face is now inside the museum and a new clock was erected to serve the town in October 2001.

During World War Two, the official 'Report Centre' was at the 'Warden's Post' at the Town Hall. Members of the Invasion Committee had to report to the Warden's Post before going on duty, to collect information as to the present state of emergency, and then afterwards to report back. The F in a broken circle, to the right of the door, is a Feudry Limit sign, indicating to prisoners of war from the camp at Sudeley that they were not allowed to go any further.

In May 1999, a time capsule was buried under the Town Hall, while the building was being repaired and restored.

# Abbey Terrace

The car park in the centre of town has its own rich history. Originally, it was part of the abbey grounds. Hearsay evidence places King Coenwulf's 'palace' or administrative centre at the east end of the terrace where the building society now stands. The road skirting round the abbey was only three metres wide in places, with a sharp double bend at the junction with Cowl Lane. In 1835, it was decided to straighten and widen the road. The relevant section of abbey land was bought; the Small-bread Hall and an adjacent turreted hall demolished, and the high stone wall moved.

In 1887, to celebrate Queen Victoria's Golden Jubilee, Emma Dent met the cost of bringing a piped water supply from St Kenelm's well to a town main in Abbey Terrace. In May 1910, Mrs E.O. Waddingham presented a massive granite drinking fountain (see above) in memory of her husband on a very grand occasion, reported in detail in **The Evesham Journal**. This was removed in the 1950s to provide car parking space.

General Sir Ian Hamilton unveiled the war memorial, made by L. Boulton & Son, Cheltenham, on 4th August 1920 (p.67).

# Sudeley Castle

When the Dent brothers, John and William, completed their purchase of Sudeley Castle in 1837, it had been a ruin for nearly 200 years.

Originally a manor house, given in the 10$^{th}$ century by King Æthelred to his daughter on her marriage, Sudeley was fortified by John of Sudeley during the Anarchy (p.21). When John, who supported Matilda, rebelled against King Stephen, Stephen seized Sudeley and made it a royal garrison.

The castle then underwent major rebuilding in the fifteenth century. Ralph Boteler, Lord Sudeley, fought for Henry V and Henry VI in the wars against France, and he was rewarded with many responsibilities and positions of power. His only son, Thomas, died in 1459 and, when the Yorkist forces defeated Henry VI's army, Ralph's daughter-in-law, Eleanor, petitioned Edward IV for the return of her husband's property. Edward seduced her and they were married in secret by Robert Stillington, later Bishop of Bath and Wells. Ralph, anticipating becoming father-in-law to the Queen of England, enhanced Sudeley Castle magnificently. Edward, however, ignored the marriage when he was re-instated as king in 1471, and he forced Ralph Boteler to sell Sudeley because Ralph had supported the Lancastrians.

When Henry VIII came to the throne in 1509, Sudeley was still crown property. Henry VIII and Anne Boleyn stayed at Sudeley for five days in 1535, and four years later Winchcombe Abbey was dissolved.

When Henry died, Thomas Seymour secretly married Queen Katherine Parr, and, when Edward VI granted Sudeley to his uncle, Thomas, Sudeley became the home of the former Queen of England. When she died after the birth of her daughter, she was buried in the chapel. The chief mourner at her funeral was not her husband but Lady Jane Grey.

During the civil wars between Charles I and Parliament, Sudeley became the headquarters of the king when he was in Gloucestershire. The site of much conflict, the castle was slighted, or rendered useless as a military stronghold, and St Mary's church was horribly desecrated.

The castle remained a ruin, occupied only by tenant farmers and an inn called the Castle Arms, until the Dent brothers used the fortune they had made from their glove-making business to start restoring it to its former glory. When the brothers died, their nephew, John Coucher Dent, inherited the estate and the fortune. He and his wife, Emma, continued to enhance the castle, and they also took an active interest in the town (p.61).

# The Vicarage

In 1845, the vicarage in Gloucester Street was extended by Rev. John Ridout Harvey to accommodate his growing family. It had been built in 1810 by Rev. John Lates, the then incumbent. Rev. Harvey doubled the size of the house by extending forward over the front garden, almost to the street, having applied for a mortgage from a fund *'for the augmentation for the maintenance of the poor clergy'*.

However, in April 1858, Harvey was sent to the debtors' prison at Gloucester. He was sentenced to nine months imprisonment but released early and continued to serve as vicar of Winchcombe for a further thirteen years, until his death in January 1871. He was a very popular man, and it was largely due to his efforts that St Peter's Church was restored in 1872.

# The First Infant School

In 1857, William Smith provided this building as the first formally recognised infant school. His intention was not just to educate the next generation, but also to free women to go to work and lift the family out of poverty. He paid £2,500 for a building which is one of Winchcombe's most significant landmarks.

When the school was moved to Cowl Lane, the building became the town assembly rooms. In 1913, the Working Men's Club acquired the lease of the building. In May 1915, part of the building, together with the Parish Hall in Cowl Lane, was opened as a VAD hospital (p.67). During World War Two, parts for Mosquito 'planes were secretly made here. In 1946, a ceremony was held here to distribute the Fighting Forces Home-coming Gift Fund.

# Victorian letter box

Pillar boxes were first introduced in England in 1853, and wall boxes in 1857. This Victorian letter box, at the bottom of Hailes Street, is still in use. At the beginning of Victoria's reign, William Simmons had taken over from Mr Wynn as Winchcombe's postmaster. The Post Office was located in Queen's Square, in the back kitchen of The Hermitage (below), the house nearest to the Chandos alms houses.

Letters were originally brought in saddle-bags from Moreton-in-Marsh, arriving in Winchcombe at 12 o'clock and returning at 4 o'clock. Some years afterwards, Winchcombe was made a sub-office under Cheltenham, and the mail was brought from Cheltenham to Winchcombe by a walking messenger.

Anthony Trollope, the novelist, visited Winchcombe in 1851, doing his best to improve rural postal deliveries. Nevertheless, mail delivery continued to depend on foot-slogging carriers who trod the miry lanes and steep hill country around Winchcombe. James Agg was appointed a rural messenger in 1856, and he served continuously for 30 years. He vividly remembered having to trudge 'nigh up to the knees in mud' during the winter in the suitably named Dirty Lane in Gretton.

# Cattle Trough

*The Metropolitan Drinking Fountain and Cattle Trough Association* was set up in London by Samuel Gurney M.P. and Edward Thomas Wakefield, a barrister, in 1859, to provide

free drinking water. On the corner of Greet Road and Crispin Road stands this cattle trough, now used for flowers. It used to stand outside the garage on the corner of North Street and Greet Road; you can just see it in the bottom right hand corner of this postcard.

The Association also supplied the fountain in Abbey Terrace, (p.53), at Mrs Waddingham's expense, on the death of her husband, John Waddingham, J.P. and chairman of the Winchcombe bench of magistrates.

# 'North Street Brewery'

The house bearing this sign, on the corner of Chandos Street and North Street, was referred to as the brewhouse in 1865 at the trial of Richard Smith, a retired surgeon. Mr Smith had shot and killed his wife, and one of the witnesses testified that she 'knocked at the brewhouse door' for milk, as she did every day. He was committed to Broadmoor Lunatic Asylum; there was a history of insanity in his family, and he had previously been diagnosed as suffering from 'chronic insanity'.

In 1897, Nailsworth Brewery bought this house and the one next door. The site was too small for commercial brewing, so they possibly used it for bottling. In 1915, the premises were sold to Cheltenham Original Brewery, which was subsequently taken over by Flowers and then by Whitbread. Known locally as the Rope Walk, it may be that the site was used by the Brewery to make the ropes needed for the shire horses in the drays. In 1953, the premises were sold as private houses, with a covenant to prevent beer being brewed, as Whitbread owned The White Lion, now known as The Lion Inn.

# Emma Dent

In 1855, Emma Dent became mistress of Sudeley, and, as you walk around Winchcombe, you cannot miss evidence of her interest in the town. In 1865, she and her husband had the alms-houses built in Abbey Terrace.

In 1867, Dent's School was opened, next to St Peter's Church, and, in 1868, she had a new church built at Gretton. Mrs Dent also restored and enlarged Jacobean House and had Three Gables rebuilt. She paid for the restoration of the Pilgrims' Gallery at the George Inn (p.27).

In 1887, to commemorate Queen Victoria's Golden Jubilee, she supplied Winchcombe with its first piped water supply from St Kenelm's Well to Abbey Terrace (p.53).

She was responsible for excavations of Roman villas at Wadfield Farm and Spoonley Villa, and she had the early excavation at Belas Knap tidied up. It was her decision to build the dry stone wall around the site, using slates that had been used by the Neolithic builders to support the revetment, the retaining wall (p.7). Originally, the monument had been disguised as a grassy mound.

# Toll Gates

Anchor House, on the corner of North Street and Back Lane, was built in 1863, around the weighbridge office. The door to the office is in the bottom left hand corner of the side view of the house (below).

The same toll keeper operated the gates on Gretton Road and Greet Road, as well as the weighbridge, which showed the weight of the load so that he could calculate the toll payable. The weighbridge was shown on the Ordnance Survey map in 1883, but it had disappeared by 1900; the workings had been removed and the underground tunnel which

housed the machinery covered up. The original name of the house derives from the trade mark of the public weighbridge.

The eastern approach to the town was gated at 'Footbridge Gate', with one gate on the Broadway Road and the other at the foot of Stancombe Lane. On the western entry, the toll gate and the toll keeper's cottage were situated at the junction with Corndean Lane.

# Cottage Hospital

The building on the far right of this photograph of North Street is the former Cottage Hospital. This was built by John Oakey, using stone given by Lord Elcho, in 1888, with money raised by local subscription. The main driving force behind the initiative was Dr William Cox, who managed to obtain promises of support from many of the more affluent residents in the neighbourhood.

When the 'new' hospital opened on Cheltenham Road in 1928, the Cottage Hospital was converted into flats and the name erased from the frontage. However, Winchcombe's coat of arms is still visible above what used to be the door.

Winchcombe Hospital closed in 2008 and was sold in 2013 to help pay for a new hospital in Tewkesbury.

# Police Station

In 1900, the county council commissioned the building of the new police station at the Anchor crossroads, which included accommodation for holding the county court, the magistrates' court and cells for prisoners.

**NEW POLICE COURT AT WINCHCOMBE.**
EXTERIOR OF NEW POLICE-COURT.

The Court is the new portion in the rear of the Police-station. The public entrance is at back, up an exterior staircase. The prisoners' staircase can also be seen, guarded by spikes. The magistrates' and solicitors' entrance is at the front.

[Photo by Cheltenham Newspaper Co., Ltd.]

This announcement of the opening of the new police court appeared in the *Cheltenham & Gloucester Gazette in 1913*.

The building has since been converted to residential use.

# Murder Alley

This alleyway in Hailes Street is known locally as 'Murder Alley', because, in 1904, Thomas Wallins, a worker on the new Cheltenham – Honeybourne railway, cut the throat of his landlord's daughter, Louisa Bingham, and then cut his own. It was revealed at the inquest that he had been stalking the young lady, but she had been doing her best to discourage his attentions. It seems likely that, when he entered the house and found her writing a love letter to his brother, he was overcome with a fit of jealousy.

This photograph was taken at the back of the house.

It shows Sarah Nash, a neighbour, standing by the door where there is a pool of blood on the ground. The victim's mother, Mrs Robins, is standing near the policeman, behind the table where Wallins cut his own throat before following Louisa into the alley.

# Winchcombe Railway Station

Winchcombe Railway Station was opened on 1st February, 1905, although there was no passenger service until 1908. The passenger service was withdrawn in 1960 and the Honeybourne to Cheltenham Line was only used for freight. In 1976, a coal train derailment near Greet caused so much damage to the track that it was decided to close it for good. The track was lifted and the buildings demolished.

When the line was re-opened in 1987, a replacement station had been brought from Monmouth Troy. All that remains of the original Winchcombe Station is the weighbridge.

# War

In 1920, a memorial was erected in Abbey Terrace to honour those local men who had died serving their country during the Great War. After the Second World War, more names were added. In St Peter's Church and in Winchcombe Museum, there are folders, researched by Carol Harris, containing a lot of information about our local heroes.

On the wall of the Working Men's Club is a plaque which commemorates the contribution made by Winchcombe in caring for sick and wounded soldiers during the First World War (p. 57). Dr John Halliwell and Eleanor Adlard established a Voluntary Aid Detachment in Winchcombe, and courses were run to train volunteers to act as nurses and stretcher bearers. Eliza Wedgwood was appointed Commandant from October 1915. The hospital opened in May, 1915, with 45 beds in two wards; the other one was in the Parish Hall in Cowl Lane (p.46). A total of 809 patients were cared for, and the town did a lot to entertain the men, providing concerts and amateur dramatic productions.

Queen Mary visited Winchcombe and Sudeley in 1922, and she stayed at Sudeley in 1934. In August, 1944, she came to Winchcombe again, to visit a 'factory'; this was almost certainly the Working Men's Club, where parts for wooden Mosquito planes were being secretly made. The finished parts were collected under cover of darkness!

During the Second World War, Winchcombe people played host to hundreds of evacuees. Those who could not be accommodated in families were given beds in the W.I. hall in Cowl Lane, originally the Methodist Chapel (p.46).

Various army units underwent training in the district, and, eventually, a purpose-built military camp was established in the Sudeley Castle grounds. During the months leading to D-Day in June 1944, U.S. troops were accommodated at Toddington manor as part of the huge invasion and supply forces being assembled for the Normandy landings. There was a prisoner of war camp established at Sudeley, and many of the prisoners worked on local farms, played football against local teams and generally made friends with Winchcombe people. The Congregational Union Church in Gretton Road (p.48) became a temporary drill hall for a platoon of the Home Guard.

Greet

Practical steps were taken to hinder any invader's progress. Signposts, milestones etc. were removed and pill boxes were erected. Some of them still survive.

Pill boxes were small forts constructed out of local stone – basically a type of dug-out or bunker with look-outs and small slits for machine guns.

Langley Road

They were strung out in lines across the landscape; each box was linked to the next by defensive ditches deep enough to stop a tank, or by natural features such as rivers.

Corndean Lane

Thankfully, Winchcombe town was relatively unscathed by the war, but nineteen men from the town had been killed on active service. Their names were added to the war memorial. 122 men and women did return to Winchcombe, and they were presented with a cheque in gratitude (p.57).

# Since the war

Since the war, the population of Winchcombe has more than doubled, aided by considerable house building; new schools, a medical centre and industrial estates have been built to meet their needs.

Virtually the whole of Winchcombe's historic core was designated a conservation area in 1971, and the town also lies within the 582 square miles of the Cotswolds which were designated an area of outstanding natural beauty in 1966.

However, since the end of the war, some significant landmarks have been lost. The seventeenth century Chandos Grammar School, the Victorian workhouse and the flour mill (below), which dated back to the time of the abbey, have been demolished; the jam factories and many of the orchards and farms have gone.

Nevertheless, the Victorian Town Hall (p.51) in the very centre of town has been repaired and given new life as home to Winchcombe's museum; the George Inn, Dent's School, the Police Station and the former Methodist Chapel in Cowl Lane have been converted to residential use, preserving much of their original appearance.

New attractions have been opened within easy reach of Winchcombe. In the grounds of the Jacobean manor house at Stanway, about four miles away, there is the tallest gravity-fed fountain in the world, powered by a tributary of the River Isbourne, as well as a working thirteenth century flour mill. About three miles away from Winchcombe is the Prescott Speed Hill Climb, at the home of the Bugatti Owners' Club.

The railway station (p.66) was lost in 1976, but the Gloucestershire Warwickshire Steam Railway Society was formed in the same year with the aim of restoring the rail link from Cheltenham to Stratford-upon-Avon, and a replacement station was opened in 1987. At the time of writing, the line reaches from Cheltenham race course to Broadway.

There is a powerful feeling in Winchcombe that its fascinating history should be cherished. Dedicated volunteers work at the museum to preserve and disseminate details of Winchcombe's past and the stories of its people. Local traditions such as Morris dancing, mummers' plays and the St Kenelm Miracle Play are being enthusiastically revived.

**The St Kenelm Miracle players in procession**

The Flower Show, which used to be such an important event in Winchcombe's calendar, was revived after the war, and, until the intervention of the pandemic in 2020, has had a continuous record of 70 shows since its revival in 1950. New traditions, such as the Music and Arts Festival and the Walking Festival, have also been interrupted because of Covid 19, but they will all resume with renewed energy when it is safe to do so.

Throughout the pandemic, Winchcombe streets have remained busy because it lies at the centre of a network of footpaths, through this area of outstanding natural beauty, which links some of the landmarks in this book. These walks, along with many places to visit, can all be found on the Winchcombe Welcomes Walkers website.

The Winchcombe Way, for instance, is a 42-mile figure-of-eight trail centred on Winchcombe. The waymarked trail is designed to show walkers the hidden gems of the northern Cotswolds. The landscape is constantly changing and reveals historic houses and provides spectacular views.

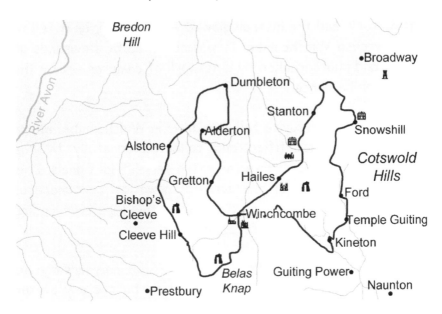

It may be that Winchcombe's glory days are behind her, but people are still eager to move into the town. The town's popularity is not only due to its rich history and beautiful surroundings; Winchcombe boasts a vast range of clubs, societies, associations and groups which cater for all manner of cultural, social, spiritual, charitable, and sports activities which help to enrich the community's life.

There are many talented people living in the area, so who knows what glories lie ahead?

73

# The Winchcombe Meteorite

At 21:54, on 28th February 2021, a meteoroid entered the earth's atmosphere travelling about 40 times faster than the speed of sound. It heated up, due to the resistance of the air on the rock, and the meteor glowed very brightly as it fell to Earth around Winchcombe. It was observed by thousands of people and photographed by a network of cameras set by the UK Fireball Alliance.

A part of the meteorite fell on a drive in Winchcombe, where it was quickly identified and collected carefully by the Wilcock family to preserve the extra-terrestrial signals. It is a very rare type of meteorite, known as **carbonaceous chondrite;** there is no record of one of this type ever landing in the United Kingdom before.

It was part of a parent body formed 4.6 billion years ago, at the very beginning of our Solar System, before any of the planets - including Earth! It is like a fossil record of the evolution of planets, so it might reveal secrets about the processes and events that led to the birth of our world. It might offer clues about where water came from and provide the answer to why it is possible for plants and animals to live on Earth.

In August 2021, the Wilcock family donated some of the meteorite to the Winchcombe Museum, where it is kept in a desiccator, with oxygen scavengers to maintain a constant humidity. We are grateful to scientists from the Natural History Museum in London for helped in creating the display.

From a video by Ben Stanley, processed by Marcus Kempf, the AllSky7 Network

**Above:** The fireball streaking through the sky.

**Below:** the meteorite on display in Winchcombe Museum

# Further Reading

Adlard, E. (1939) *Winchcombe Cavalcade*, E.J. Burrow

Bray, J. (2000) *The Lady of Sudeley,* Long Barn Books

Butler, Bert (1984) *A Cotswold Rag-Bag,* Sue Ryder Foundation

Crow, A. (2015) *Weird and Wicked Winchcombe,* Winchcombe Folk and Police Museum

Dent, E. (1877) *Annals of Sudeley and Winchcombe*, John Murray

Donaldson, D.N. (2001) *Winchcombe: A History of the Cotswold borough,* The Wychwood Press

Haigh, Gordon (1947) *The History of Winchcombe Abbey,* Skeffington and Son

Herod, Alan (2020) *Winchcombe Flower Show – A History,* Winchcombe Museum

Lovatt, Mike (2012) *The River Isbourne in the Service of Mankind,* Amberley Publishing

Meurig-Davies, Rev. T.T. (1939) *Handbook to Winchcombe Parish Church*

Oakey, J. (1937) *Reminiscences of Winchcombe*, Winchcombe Town Trust

Stevinson, Jo (2003) *Ralph Boteler, Lord Sudeley c. 1391-1473*

Stevinson, John (2005/6) *History of Winchcombe Abbey*

Stevinson, John (2005) *The Changing Face Of St Peter's*

*www.winchcombewelcomeswalkers.com*

Winkless, D. (1990) *Hailes Abbey, Gloucestershire,* Spredden Press

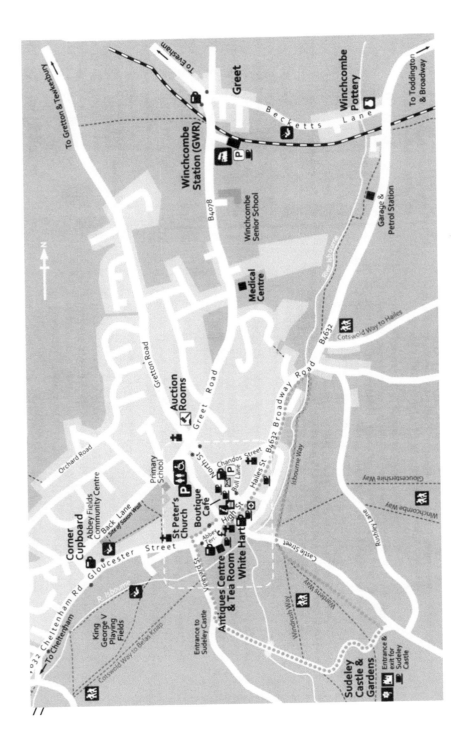